She Dreams, She Achieves

A Women's Vision Board

Clip Art Book

Healthy Food

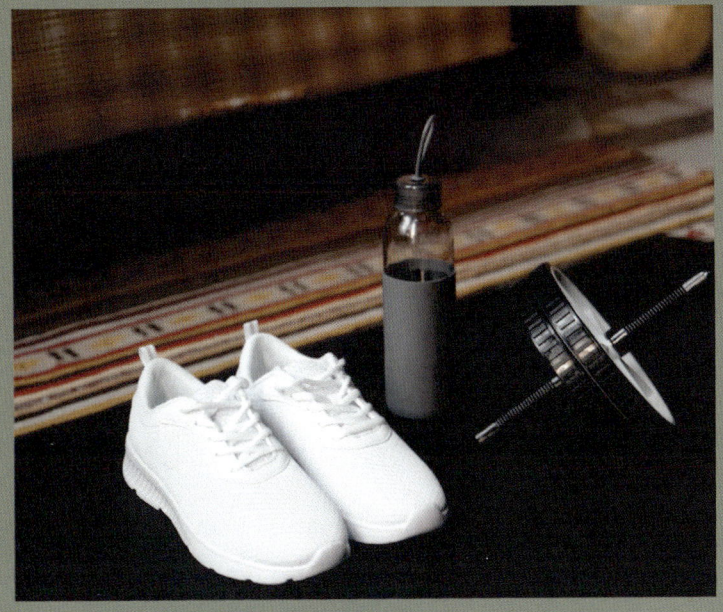

I'M WORKING OUT NOT TO BE SKINNY BUT TO BE FIT

This Girl Loves To Dance

Just Dance

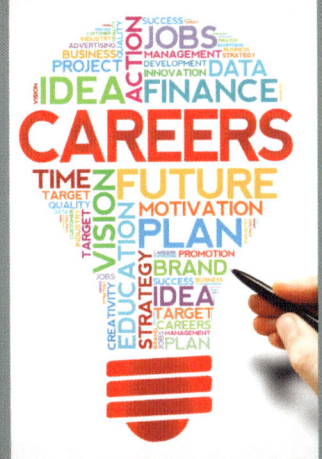

SURFER GIRL

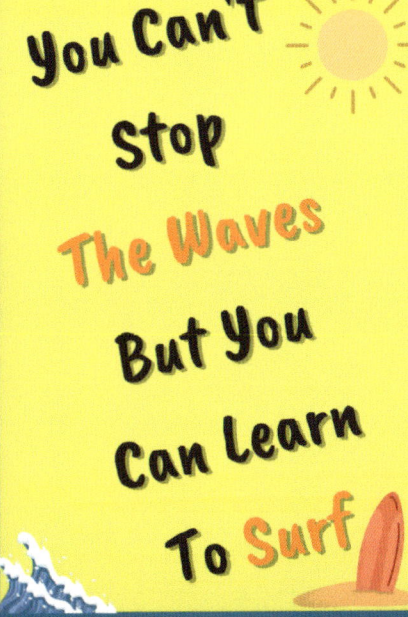

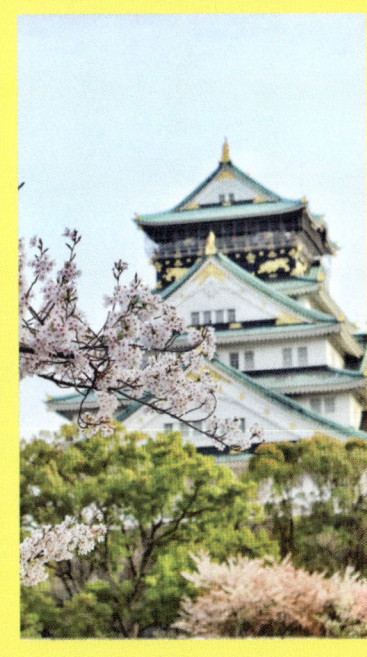

It's Time For a New Adventure

So Much World So Little Time

HAPPINESS IS RECEIVING WHAT YOU ORDERERD ONLINE

I Could Give Up Shopping But I am Not a Quitter

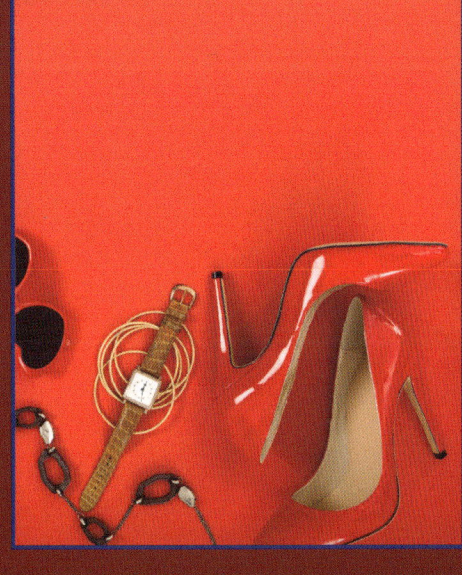

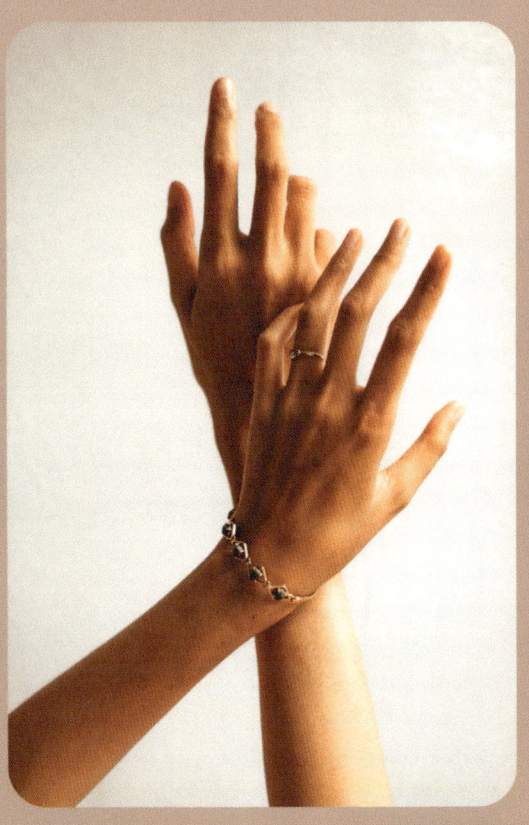

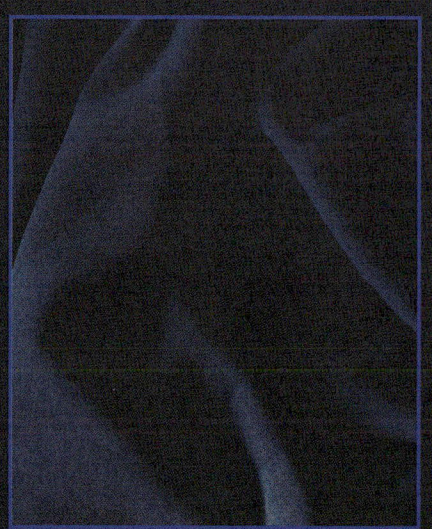